W9-AJX-509

Titles in This Set

Under My Hat

Hurry, Furry Feet

Our Singing Planet

My Favorite Foodles

Happy Faces

A Canary with Hiccups

About the Cover
Gary Baseman drew the pictures on the cover of this
book. He has been drawing ever since he was little. He
liked doodling so much that he decided to make
illustrating his job.

ISBN 0-673-80012-1

Copyright © 1993
Scott, Foresman and Company, Glenview, Illinois
All Rights Reserved.
Printed in the United States of America.

This publication is protected by Copyright and
permission should be obtained from the publisher
prior to any prohibited reproduction, storage in a
retrieval system, or transmission in any form or by
any means, electronic, mechanical, photocopying,
recording, or otherwise. For information regarding
permission, write Scott, Foresman and Company,
1900 East Lake Avenue, Glenview, Illinois 60025.

CELEBRATE READING! ® is a registered trademark of
Scott, Foresman and Company.

Acknowledgments appear on page 128.

345678910 VHJ 99989796959493

Hurry, Furry Feet

ScottForesman
A Division of HarperCollinsPublishers

INSTRUCTIONAL RESOURCE CENTER
Evergreen School District 114
2205 N.E. 138 Avenue
Vancouver, WA 98684-7228

Contents

Meet These Feet!

My Neighborhood

Small to Tall

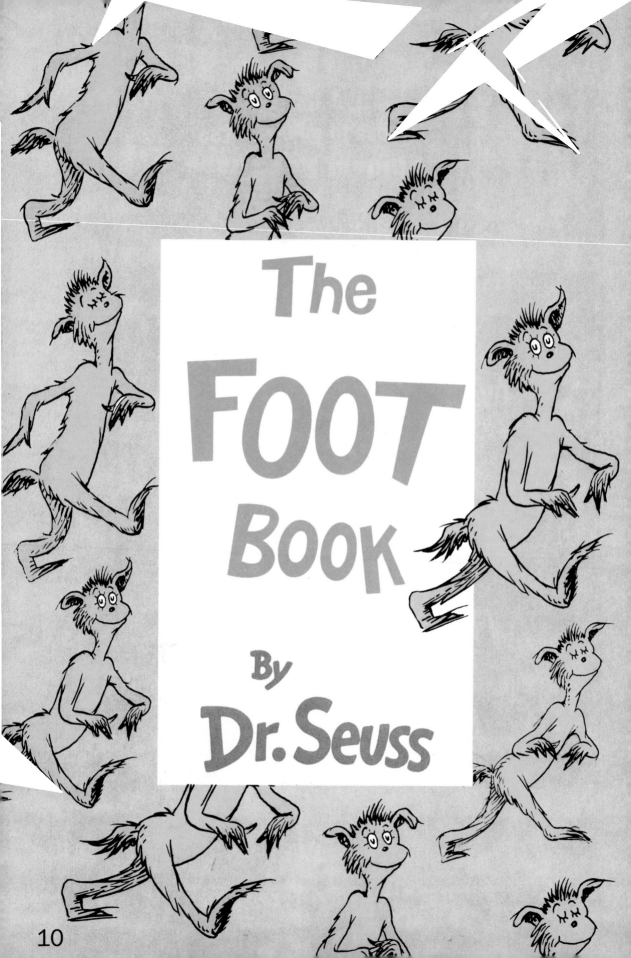

The FOOT BOOK

By Dr. Seuss

11

Slow feet

Quick feet

Trick feet

Sick feet

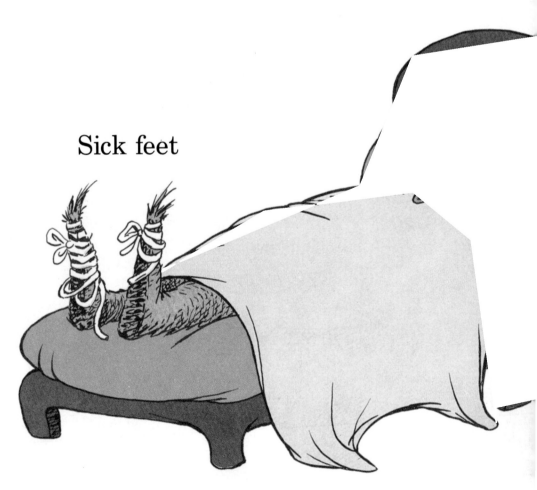

Up feet

Down feet

Here come clown feet.

Small feet

Big feet

Here come pig feet.

His feet

Her feet

Fuzzy fur feet

In the house,
and on the street,

how many, many
feet you meet.

Up in the air feet

Over a chair feet

More and more feet

Twenty-four feet

Here come
more and **more** . . . .

. . . . and **more** feet!

Left foot.   Right foot.

Feet. Feet. Feet.

Oh, how many
feet you meet!

29

Hurry, Hurry, Hurry!

by Dr. Seuss

Two legs, four legs, six legs, eight!
We all have to hurry or we'll all be late.
Hurry, hurry, hurry, or we'll all be late!
Two legs, four legs, six legs, eight!

But when you hurry fast, you begin to puff and blow.
And your legs won't last, so we'd better hurry slow.
So let's be late, that's what we'll do,
With our eight legs, six legs, four legs, two!

Parade

by Harriet Ziefert

illustrations by Saul Mandel

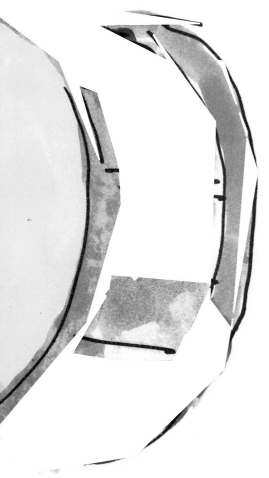

A parade!
A parade!
I know a parade
by the sound of the drum.

A-rum-a-tee-tum!
A-rum-a-tee-tum!

Here it comes
down the street.

I know a parade
by the sound
of the feet.

Music and feet.
Music and feet.

Can't you feel
the sound
and the beat?

A-rum-a-tee-tum!
A-rum-a-tee-tum!

Here comes a clown
down the street.

I know a clown
by the nose and the feet.

Here comes an elephant
down the street.

I know an elephant
by its trunk and its feet.

Here come horses down the street.
Music and feet. Music and feet.

Can't you feel the sound and the beat?
A-rum-a-tee-tum! A-rum-a-tee-tum!

A-rum-a-tee
rum-a-tee
rum-a-tee-tum!

Jump or Jiggle

by Evelyn Beyer

Frogs jump.
Caterpillars hump.

Worms wiggle.
Bugs jiggle.

Rabbits hop.
Horses clop.

Snakes slide.
Sea gulls glide.

Mice creep.
Deer leap.

Puppies bounce.
Kittens pounce.

Lions stalk—

but—
I walk!

Where Is Bravo?

by Cecilia Avalos

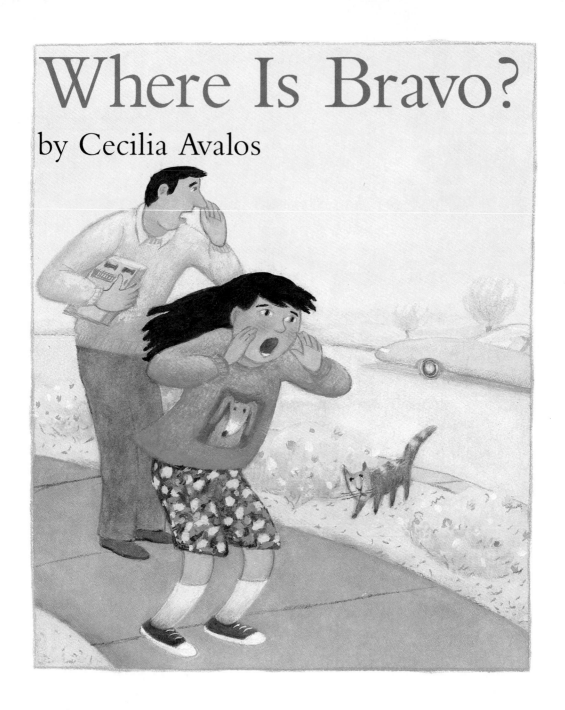

Where is Bravo?
Where, oh where?

We don't see him
anywhere.

Flippy, floppy go our feet,
to look for Bravo
down the street.

People and cars
are here and there.

Trucks and buses
are everywhere!

We don't know
where Bravo can be.

So home we go,
my Daddy and me.

THERE is Bravo,
waiting for me!

My Street Begins at My House

by Ella Jenkins

illustrations by James E. Ransome

My street begins at my house.
My street begins at my house.
My street begins at my house.
It's a very special street.

On my street things go up and down.
On my street things go 'round and 'round.
On my street things go upside down.
It's a very special street.

Some streets go one way.

Some streets go two ways.

Some streets lead to the highway.

And some streets go EVERYWHERE.

My street begins at my house.
My street begins at my house.
My street begins at my house.
It's a very special street.

My Street

by Ella Jenkins

Ella L. Jenkins

When I was a child, I lived on the South
Side of Chicago.

What made **my street** special was:
my friends, the candy store,
the shoeshine shop (they made shoes there),
the church across the street, and the many,
many cars, cabs, and trucks that passed my
house each day.

I thought about my special street when I
wrote my song.

If you wrote a song about your street,
what would you write?

62

Photo: Gwendolen Cates

63

Stop—Go

by Dorothy Baruch

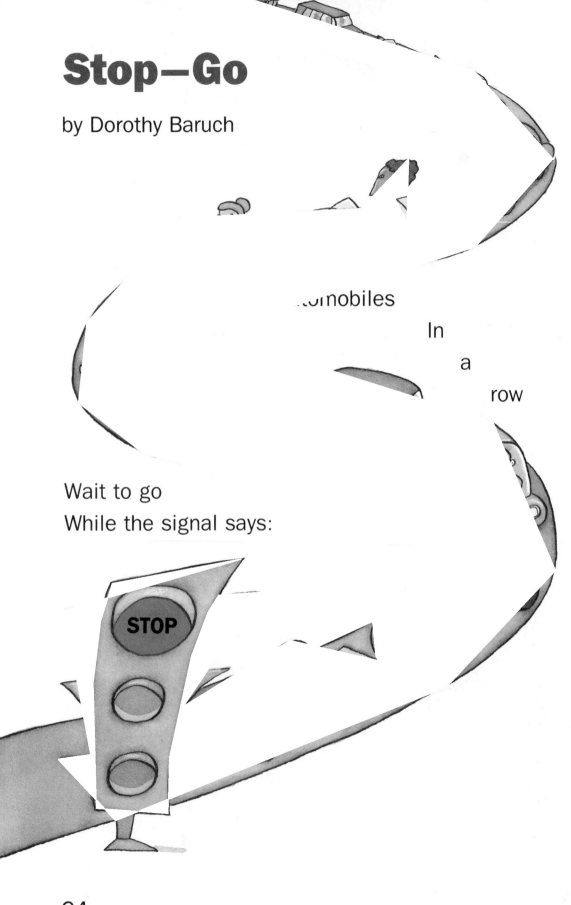

...omobiles

In

a

row

Wait to go
While the signal says:

STOP

Bells ring
Tingaling
Red light's gone!
Green light's on!
Horns blow!
And the row

Starts

to

GO

The wheels on the bus go 'round and 'round,
  'round and 'round, 'round and 'round.
The wheels on the bus go 'round and 'round,
  all around the town.

The driver on the bus says, "Move on back!"
"Move on back!" "Move on back!"
The driver on the bus says, "Move on back!"
all around the town.

The people on the bus go up and down,
  up and down, up and down.
The people on the bus go up and down,
  all around the town.

The baby on the bus says, "Wah, wah, wah!"
"Wah, wah, wah!" "Wah, wah, wah!"
The baby on the bus says, "Wah, wah, wah!"
all around the town.

The parents on the bus say, "Shh, shh, shh!"
"Shh, shh, shh!" "Shh, shh, shh!"
The parents on the bus say, "Shh, shh, shh!"
  all around the town.

The people on the bus step off the bus,
off the bus, off the bus.
The people on the bus step off the bus,
all around the town.

Small to Tall

When the Elephant Walks

by Keiko Kasza

When the Elephant walks . . .

he scares the Bear.

When the Bear runs away. . .

he scares the Crocodile.

When the Crocodile swims for his life . . .

he scares the Wild Hog.

When the Wild Hog dashes for safety. . .

he scares Mrs. Raccoon.

When Mrs. Raccoon flees with her baby . . .

they scare the little Mouse.

But when the little Mouse scurries in terror . . .

. . . Well, who would be scared by a little Mouse?

A Note from Keiko Kasza

Have you ever been afraid of something?

All of us know how that feels.
That is why I decided to write a story about it.
I wanted children to know that we all get scared.
Even the mighty elephant in my story is afraid of
something!

The next time you feel afraid, remember there may
be someone bigger than you who gets scared too!

Un elefante

Un elefante se balanceaba
sobre la tela de una araña.
Como veía que resistía,
fue a llamar a un camarada.

An elephant was balancing
upon a spider's web.
When he saw that it was strong enough,
he went to call a friend.

Dos elefantes se balanceaban
sobre la tela de una araña.
Como veían que resistía,
fueron a llamar a un camarada.

Two elephants were balancing
upon a spider's web.
When they saw that it was strong enough,
they went to call a friend.

Tres elefantes se balanceaban
sobre la tela de una araña.
Como veían que resistía,
fueron a llamar a un camarada.

Three elephants were balancing
upon a spider's web.
When they saw that it was strong enough,
they went to call a friend.

Cuatro elefantes se balanceaban
sobre la tela de una araña.
Como veían que resistía,
fueron a llamar a un camarada.

Four elephants were balancing
upon a spider's web.
When they saw that it was strong enough,
they went to call a friend.

Sitting in My Box

by Dee Lillegard
illustrations by Jon Agee

Sitting in my box.

A tall giraffe knocks.

''Let me, let me in.''
 So I move over.

Sitting in my box.
An old gray
elephant knocks.

"Let me, let me in."
So we both
move over.

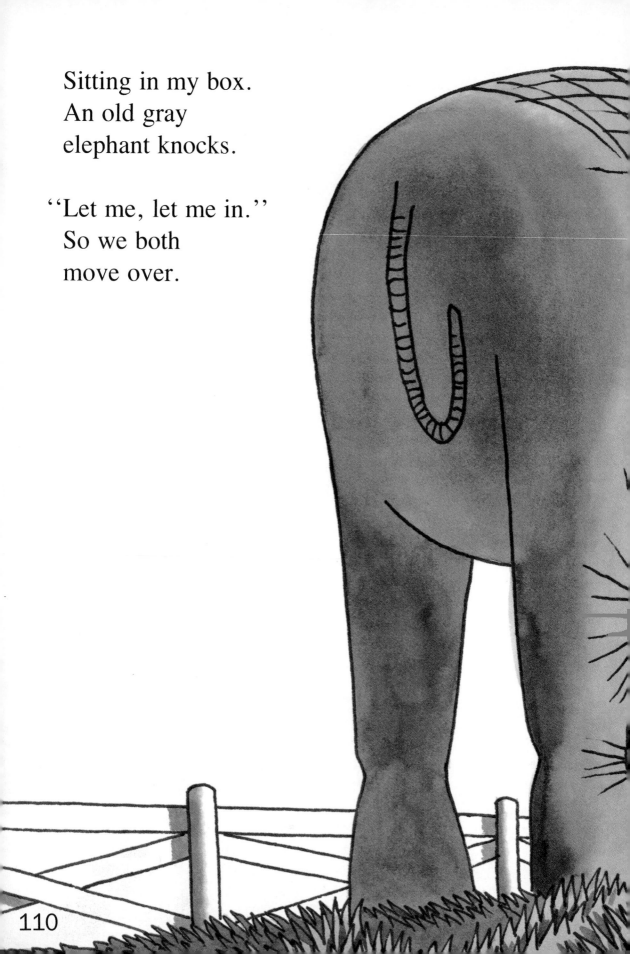

Sitting in my box.
A big baboon knocks.

"Let me, let me in."
So we all move over.

Sitting in my box.
A grumpy lion knocks.

"Let me, let me in."
So we all move over.

Sitting in my box.
A hippopotamus knocks.

"Let me, let me in."
So we *all* move over.

Standing in my box.
There's no room to sit.

"Wait a minute!
This box has
too much in it."

"Someone has to go."

"Not me."

"Not me.

"Not me."

"Not me."

"Not me."

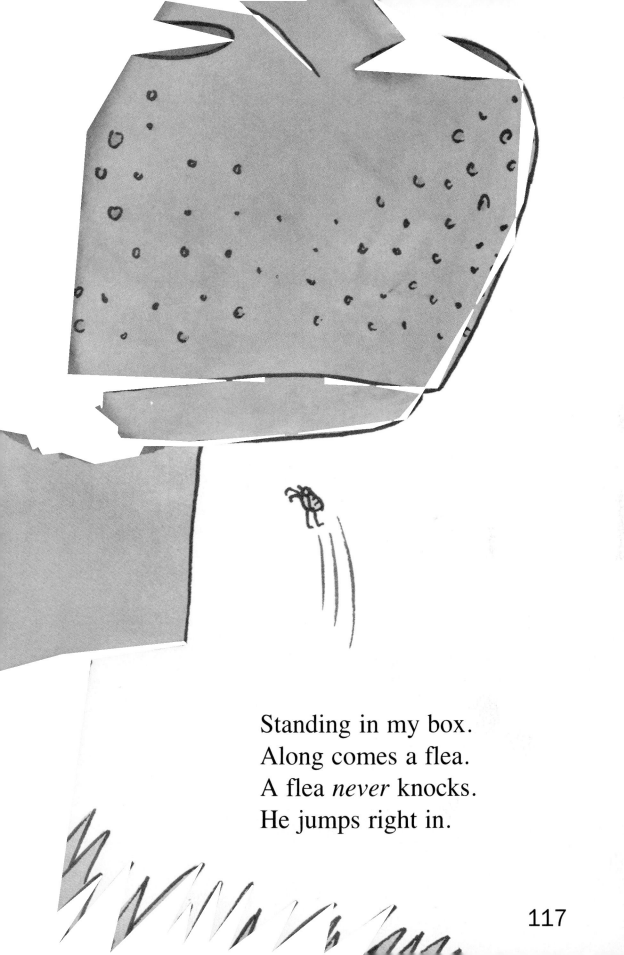

Standing in my box.
Along comes a flea.
A flea *never* knocks.
He jumps right in.

117

He bites the hippo
and the grumpy lion.

He bites the baboon
and the old gray elephant.

He bites the tall giraffe.

That's why I'm
sitting in my box . . .

just me.

Books to Enjoy

Shoes

by Elizabeth Winthrop
Illustrations by William Joyce

There are shoes to skate in and
shoes to skip in. What are the
best shoes for you?

Hooray for Snail!

by John Stadler

Wow! Small Snail hits a baseball
to the moon. Find out if that gives
him enough time to make a home run.

Green Eggs and Ham

by Dr. Seuss

Would you eat green eggs and ham?
Would you eat them on a train? In the
rain? Sam-I-am thinks you'll like them.

Flying
by Donald Crews

Get ready for take-off! See the sights as this airplane flies from the city to the country and back again.

I Walk and Read
by Tana Hoban

This book takes you on a reading walk. You might see some of these signs in your neighborhood.

How Joe the Bear and Sam the Mouse Got Together
by Beatrice Schenk de Regniers
Illustrations by Bernice Myers

Find out what a big bear and a little mouse like to do together.

Pictionary
Things We Do with Our Feet

jump

kick

skip

dance

march

run

splash

climb

Animals

raccoon

camel

bear

crocodile

elephant

hippopotamus

snail

spider

Acknowledgments

Text

Page 10: From *The Foot Book* by Dr. Seuss. Copyright © 1968 by Theodor S. Geisel and Audrey S. Geisel. Reprinted by permission of Random House, Inc.

Page 30: The song "Hurry, Hurry, Hurry!" and the illustrations from "The Super-Supper March" were originally published in *The Cat in the Hat Songbook* by Dr. Seuss. Music by Eugene Poddany. Copyright © 1967 by Theodor S. Geisel and Audrey S. Geisel and Eugene Poddany. Reprinted by permission of Random House, Inc.

Page 32: *Parade* by Harriet Ziefert. Illustrated by Saul Mandel. Copyright © 1990 by Harriet Ziefert. Illustrations copyright © 1990 by Saul Mandel. Used by permission of Bantam, a division of Bantam Doubleday Dell Publishing Group, Inc.

Page 42: "Jump or Jiggle" by Evelyn Beyer, from *Another Here and Now Story Book* by Lucy Sprague Mitchell. Copyright © 1937 by E. P. Dutton, renewed © 1965 by Lucy Sprague Mitchell. Used by permission of Dutton Children's Books, a division of Penguin Books USA Inc.

Page 52: *Where Is Bravo?* by Cecilia Avalos. Copyright © 1991 by Cecilia Avalos.

Page 58: "My Street Begins at My House" by Ella Jenkins. Words and music by Ella Jenkins. Copyright © 1971 by Ella Jenkins. Reprinted by permission of Ell-Bern Publishing Company.

Page 62: "My Street" by Ella Jenkins. Copyright © 1991 by Ella Jenkins.

Page 64: "Stop—Go" from *I Like Automobiles* by Dorothy Baruch. Permission granted by Bertha Klausner International Literary Agency, Inc.

Page 74: *When the Elephant Walks,* written and illustrated by Keiko Kasza, copyright © 1990 by Keiko Kasza. Reprinted by permission of G. P. Putnam's Sons.

Page 101: "A Note from Keiko Kasza" by Keiko Kasza. Copyright © 1991 by Keiko Kasza.

Page 102: "Un elefante" Traditional. English translation by Sharon, Lois and Bram. Copyright © 1981 Pachyderm Music, Elephant Records. Reprinted by permission of Elephant Records.

Page 106: *Sitting in My Box* by Dee Lillegard. Illustrated by Jon Agee. Text copyright © 1989 by Dee Lillegard. Illustrations copyright © 1989 by Jon Agee. Used by permission of Dutton Children's Books, a division of Penguin Books USA, Inc.

Artists

Illustrations owned and copyrighted by the illustrator.
Gary Baseman, 1–9, 50–51, 72–73, 122–127
Theodor S. Geisel, 10–29, 30–31
Saul Mandel, 32–41
Roni Shepherd, 52–57
James E. Ransome, 58–61
Richard A. Goldberg, 64–65
Bonnie Timmons, 66–71
Keiko Kasza, 74–100
Craig Smallish, 102–105
Jon Agee, 106–121

Photographs

Page 42: (top) Kim Taylor/Bruce Coleman, Inc. (bottom) Ron Goor/Bruce Coleman, Inc.
Page 43: (top) Andrew Rakoczy/Bruce Coleman, Inc. (bottom) Larry West/Bruce Coleman, Inc.
Page 44: (top) Roger Wilmshurst/Bruce Coleman, Inc. (bottom) Fritz Prenzel/Bruce Coleman, Inc.
Page 45: (top) Phil Degginger/Bruce Coleman, Inc. (bottom) Roger Wilmshurst/Bruce Coleman, Inc.
Page 46: (top) Joe McDonald/Bruce Coleman, Inc. (bottom) Leonard Lee Rue III/Bruce Coleman, Inc.
Page 47: (top) Walter Chandoha (bottom) Bruce McMillan
Page 48: G. Schaller/Bruce Coleman, Inc.
Page 49: David Kent Madison/Bruce Coleman, Inc.
Page 63: Gwendolen Cates
Page 101: Courtesy of Keiko Kasza.